Poet in the House!

CK C
gll.54
c.1
9/18

Poet in the House!
© *Copyright Broadside Press 2005*
International Standard Book Number 0940713-15-2
Library of Congress Control Number: 2005907876

michigan council for
arts and cultural affairs

City of Detroit
CULTURAL AFFAIRS
DEPARTMENT

Poet in the House!

The Poet-in-Residence Program:
A Decade of Collaboration between
Broadside Press and the Detroit Public Library

Gloria House, Semaj Brown, and Willie Williams
Editors

Broadside Press
Detroit

Dedicated to

Dudley and Vivian Randall

and

Hilda and Don Vest

PHOTO BY WILLIE WILLIAMS

Dudley Randall (1914 - 2000)
Founder of Broadside Press

CONTENTS

PHOTO BY MONICA MORGAN

Hilda and Don Vest, Broadside Publishers, 1985–1998

When Don and Hilda Vest assumed ownership of Broadside Press from its founder, Dudley Randall, the excitement of the Black consciousness and Black arts movements had subsided considerably. Those movements of the 1960's and '70's had generated an unparalleled mushrooming of literary production in Black communities throughout the world. However, in 1985 when the Vests took over the Press, Randall warned sadly: "Hilda, nobody buys poetry."

The Vests understood that the Press would not make a fortune; profit was not their motive. Theirs was a commitment to the extraordinary African American literary legacy that Randall had established through his singular determination and exhausting discipline. The Vests would go on to publish 14 titles during their ownership of Broadside, upholding the reputation for excellent poetry, and adding to the impressive repertory that Randall had built – one which included the first or early publications of every nationally acclaimed contemporary African American poet, including Haki Madhubuti, Sonia Sanchez, Nikki Giovanni, Etheridge Knight and Audre Lorde, as well as the poems and autobiography of Pulitzer Prize winner, Gwendolyn Brooks.

While publishing new poets and continuing Broadside cultural events and workshops, the Vests were asking themselves how the Press might offer concrete support to poets beyond the sale of their books. In answer to this question, Don Vest, who was then a member the Board of the Friends of the Detroit Library (Friends DPL), developed the idea of creating Broadside Press collaborations with other cultural and educational institutions, and seeking funds in order to be able to offer stipends to poets to serve the community through these institutions.

The pilot for the many collaborations to come was a project called "To Dream a Book," which was implemented in partnership with the Friends DPL Executive Director Paul Scupholm and Jim Evenhuis, then in charge of the DPL Westside libraries. The first site was Duffield Library, where there was a very strong Friends group led by Mr. and Mrs. Albert Mallory. The Duffield Friends carried out vigorous fundraising efforts in the churches and local businesses, and had the support and cooperation of their entire neighborhood. Thus Duffield Library provided the perfect community context for the Vests' pilot venture. The children from Thirkell Elementary School came to Duffield Library for sessions of poetry appreciation and writing. At the end of several weeks, the children's writings and drawings were collected in a publication entitled *To Dream a Book*. A second pilot, organized similarly, involved Sherrard Elementary School children and Knapp Library. In both of these experimental ventures, Hilda Vest was the poet/teacher/facilitator.

Having seen the ways in which these projects benefited the children and the schools while enhancing use of the libraries, the Vests were ready to launch the full-scale enterprise that became the Poet-In-Residence Program (PIR). With the assistance of Scupholm and Evenhuis, they acquired funding from Comerica Bank and a matching grant from the Michigan Council for Arts and Cultural Affairs (MCACA). In the initial Poet-In-Residence Program, Broadside placed 20 poets in 15 Detroit and five suburban libraries to conduct workshops on poetry appreciation and writing. The sessions were conducted during the months of May through August, with the poets receiving stipends of $100 per session, which compensated them for workshop preparation, instruction, travel, and copy/duplication expenses. The model worked successfully, and more residencies were added each summer, in out-state libraries as far as Saginaw, and in senior centers as well.

In 1990, Broadside Press extended its programmatic support of writers by successfully pursuing grants from the Neighborhood Opportunity Fund, the Detroit Department of Cultural Affairs, and New Detroit, Inc. Using the PIR model, the Vests started programs for special populations in non-traditional settings: "Poetry as a Second Language" (poetry as therapy) placed a poet in residence at Sobriety House, Mariners' Inn and Harbor Light Center, with the objective of helping participants as they struggled to overcome their addictions. Poet Ron Allen was instrumental in developing and sustaining "Poetry as a Second

Language." The "Vision of Words" project assigned poets to work with troubled adolescents and teens at Boysville, the Detroit Detention Center, Alternative for Girls and the Catherine Ferguson Academy. Poets Aurora Harris and Leonard King provided leadership and inspiration for youngsters at these venues. Irene Rosemond and Anita Timbers spearheaded "Reflections," a program in which seniors shared memories and wrote about their lives, in workshops held at First Congregational Church in the Cultural Center, and Central Methodist Church in Downtown Detroit.

Over the ten-year duration of the Poet-In-Residence Program, the number of poets, libraries and other sites involved each summer ranged from 20 to 30. The poets represented multiple ethnic, racial and cultural communities, and belonged to widely differing aesthetic schools. Thus for a decade, hundreds of adults and children in dozens of neighborhoods were encouraged to develop their creativity with the inspiration and guidance of some of the most competent and culturally-diverse writers in the Detroit metropolitan area, while at the same time, they made good use of many other programs and services available in the their local libraries.

The significance of the PIR and all the programs engendered by Broadside Press under the Vests' leadership is that they situated the poet right in the heart of the community, as a working, contributing member, capable of responding creatively to the many needs of diverse constituencies, truly making a difference, and worthy of support. The PIR model rendered the Broadside Press ideal of the socially engaged writer a concrete reality.

The Vests passed on the coordination of the PIR first to Stella Crews, then to M. L. Liebler and finally to Gloria House (Aneb Kgositsile). The MCACA and the Friends continued to provide matching funds each summer till 2002, when funding cutbacks prevented the Friends from continuing their support. Throughout these years, Broadside enjoyed the enthusiastic cooperation and partnership of the Friends and the DPL administration. This publication is intended to bring the long-standing collaboration to a fitting closure.

Broadside Press is thankful to the agencies and individuals whose cooperation we have enjoyed, especially, of course, the librarians, who opened their doors to us with hospitality and enthusiasm. We would like to acknowledge Viola Taylor and Yvette Shane for their generous and warm assistance with the administrative details of scheduling, and Cheryl Sartin of Friends of DPL for accounting and processing of stipends. For funding this project, we would like to express our appreciation to Dr. James Hart and the Detroit Department of Cultural Affairs, and to the MCACA, especially to Executive Director Betty Boone, who understands so profoundly the role of artists in our communities.

We also thank all the poets and musicians who have served the Program. Many are represented in this collection. Additional participants were: Ventra Asana, Irv Barat, Heather Buchanan, Marianne Cameron, Paulette Childress, Wil Clay, Lynne Meredith Cohn, Larry Gabriel, Charles Gervin, Mary Hall, Bill Harris, Robert Haynes, Al Hellus, Murray Jackson, Leonard King, Gerry La Femma, Jahra Michelle McKinney, Ray McKinney, Ron Milner, Mary Minock, Peggy Moore, Delfin Munoz, Larry Pike, Ibn Pori-Pitts, Jane Ratcliffe, Ozzie Rivera, Irene Rosemond, Bethany Schryburt, Sharon Smith-Knight, Elizabeth Socolow, Teresa Tan, Melanie Van der Tuin, Roberto Warren, JoAnn Washington, Mary Ann Wehler andKaren Williams.

We hope you enjoy the poems we have selected from the Poets-In-Residence and the workshop participants, and that you will celebrate with us this rare, long-term collaboration between a small African American press and one of the finest city library systems in the United States. *Poet in the House!* commemorates the success of this historic undertaking.

Gloria House, Ph.D., Semaj Brown, Willie Williams
May 26, 2004

Part I

Poems by Poets-in-Residence

Several Poets-in-Residence at LeCafethe Restaurant, 2001
Front Row, l-r: Semaj Brown, Sonya Pouncy. Second Row: Stephen Jones,
Liberty Daniels, Jacqueline Sanchez, Aurora Harris, Margo LaGattuta

A group of participating writers, Poet-in-Residence 2000, outside the Broadside Press
Lafayette Street office. Left to right: Joan Gartland, Wardell Montgomery, Leslie Reese,
Willie Williams, Rod Reinhart, Liberty Daniels, Al Ward, M.L. Liebler, Murray Jack-
son, Regina Reid, Aurora Harris, Gloria House, We Clear the Land (Cynthia Henderson).

1

Breath

Sarah Addae

Fields of straw and stars made of straw,
Fields of fire and stars of fire,
A child conceiving, a star conceiving,
When they leave,
Fields of red, stars of red.
Where do they go?
Into the pulse of the _____
Into the arms of the _____
Into the heart with no geography.
Into the mother that must kiss us all with the truth
Of in and out.

dancing is flying

Melba Joyce Boyd

for jackie hillsman

dancing is flying
dancing is flying
on top of your
father's swing-tipped
steps lifting you
unto riffs and winds
of Ellington
symphonics
scaling the
liberties of
creative flight

dancing is flying
dancing is flying
with a pistol
in your purse
tight to the hip
behind the
steel door
of your studio
where rhythms
of bare feet
on the cusp
of hope and
despair meet
art liberating air
powered in
sheer, black
leotard-bodies
leaping joyfully
higher than
conspiracies
of dead effects
and fear spawned
like street corner
trash thrown

from distorted
grimaces of
pale masks

dancing is flying
dancing is flying
in experimental
movements above
submissive sterility
and a society
of gravity
and disease
that invaded
your leg
but could not
break the swing
in your father's
winged steps

we see you
dancing
we see you
flying
dancing is
flying is
dancing is
flying is
dancing
is
flying
is
dancing
is

Frederick's of Hollywood

Liberty R. O. Daniels

(for Breast Cancer Awareness Month)

two perfectly shaped beige cones

I remember looking through the catalog many times alone
underneath the cover
with the lights on
or in the bathroom with the door locked
Frederick's of Hollywood
all that sexy underwear
bordering on vulgarity
those panties with no seat in the middle
what was that about?
and those models
God
nobody is really built like that
are they?
those huge breasts
those tiny waistlines

which came first
the Frederick's catalog or the Barbie doll?
was one invented to complement the other?

some of my girlfriends started getting breasts in the 5th grade
by the end of the 6th grade everybody had them
that is everybody but me
I tried to rationalize that I was younger than most of my
friends
being that my birthday was in late September
but when I discovered that Beverly Mitchell had some
I was outdone
her birthday was in November

in the 7th grade
I took it upon myself to stop wearing undershirts
and start wearing my sister's old throw away bras
there was this one that had quilted cups
I loved it
mainly because I didn't have to stuff it with as much toilet
tissue to fill it up

by the time I reached 13
I was fed up waiting for my breasts to grow
I decided that I would never get any
why not?
my mother's breasts were huge
hung down almost to her knees
at least when she was sitting down
how come I was breast-absent?

I filled out the order blank
was proud enough to put my first, middle, and last names
down
1516 Broad Street
Flint 3, Michigan
yeah
that was before zip codes
so what!?
1516 Broad Street is now where 475 meets 69 in Flint

allow 4 to 6 weeks for delivery
ok
by the time they get here
school will be out
I'll be home
I'll have 5 dollars for the C.O.D.
and nobody will know but me

3 weeks later
my package came
I was sitting on the living room sofa watching TV
when the postman knocked on the screen door
I didn't have a dime
I asked my mother for 5 dollars
she wanted to know what for
for my package
who's it from and what's in it?
oh, God
she's not going to give me the money

my package will be returned and I'll be
breastless
the rest of my life

she made me open the plain brown wrapper
so she could see what was in it
before she handed the postman her money
I was crushed
embarrassed
my eyes lowered
and stayed affixed on the package
as I slowly opened it
very slowly
very carefully
hoping she would just pay for it and go away

she didn't

when I got the package open
I held it up
so she could peek inside
she insisted that I remove the contents
I looked at the postman
I glanced a hateful glance at my mother
who now looked 10 feet tall
as I felt less than 3 inches high

how dare she humiliate me this way

I removed the two perfectly shaped beige cones

falsies
my mother grunted
"humph"
gave the postman the 5 dollar bill
and went back into the kitchen
I ran upstairs
and hid in the closet
my new breasts clutched in my hand

Harder Options

Vievee Francis

I live here
and invite you
over and over,
the harder option
where sacrifice is
the mainstay,
the bed with broken springs
and a painful lull in the middle.
I should have chosen another
city with a less thin veneer
and nature
if I wanted to lapse
into the easy sleep
of convenience,
of clean air.
This sky bears no stars
so looking out is futile.
There is the factory
and the smudged cathedral
whose bells are off several minutes.
There are the gray rows
of houses and their tenants
sitting for dinners of sausages
and doughy children.
The television is on.
Nothing is remarkable.
Grace is a quick word
or two.
I wait for your heavy hands
and their smell of oil and habit.

Looking for Leonard Woolf

Joan Gartland

(An affirmation for women who write)

No questions asked–a cup of tea
brought up the bedroom stairs to me;
a calming hand upon my brow;
a kindly word spoke like a vow–
O, comfort, like a comforter,
how I wish that you were there!

He who'd bring me aspirin
and English muffins spread with jam;
who'd love me even when I'm mad
and tell me jokes when I am sad;
Leonard, such a saint is he,
would found a printing house for me.

Who needs a brute from some dark bar
who never heard of literature
and hates all women of renown–
even those who end up drowned.
If I should die before I wake,
Leonard's tears would not be fake.

Car Wash Man

Joan Gartland

Out of charity
he does not ask you
where you have been
or why you waited so long.
His face recedes into silence
as you drop the keys
into his hand.
Sometimes, you are sure he will say
you've waited too long–
it will never come off,
or it will take two trips
and there are too many others
lined up behind you.
But, incredibly, he does begin again–
the old maneuver with the tracks
and then the slow, neutral pull
into the dark.
You don't have to ask–
he averts his eyes
as the mud sluffs off.

What Words Are There?

Aurora Harris

For John Coltrane

A star falls

And what words are there
When walking paths

Through applause and
Conversations

Are faces becoming
Bodies

That speak without
Sound?

What words are there
When strolling into cool night air

You find
Wind does not stop

The hush of the Nile or
Detroit River

Where light of yellow flames and
Night birds fill

Empty
Where shadows are as tall

And reaching as
John?

What words are there?
What words are there?

When weightless lotus stare
At open skies

Where borderlands of sound
Rhythms and

Compositions
Inside yourself

Meet and
Become transparent sheets of

Music made from
Water sand and swirl?

What words are there
When waking traces of memories

Discover
Melancholy peace

In rows of African violets
Raging in their beauty in a

Stream of moon?
Some quiet flame

Of peace
That brought John's

Compassion

Love

Consequences

Serenity   his

Meditations inside

Interstellar Space

Where Stellar Regions are

Rattle and tremble
The cold sweat driven circular reflection

In splashes, colors
Spark, storm and

Glances of his language

Written on pages of

His being and not?

What words are there?
What words are there?
What words are there?

What doors are open in
Spaces between breeze and
Lush rich neons of
Sleeping cities?

The flow of touching rivers with eyes?
The flow of tasting a moment of sky?
The flow of standing on lightning bolts
To find an image   chord   perfect note

That only appears in brilliant flashes
That disappear like echoes
Through holes of time
That erase itself

In the middle of the world's
Insomniac nights
When waterfalls are really
Sepia sketches of flowers

Blooming along the edges of
An artist's mind?
What words are there

With that photo of John
Standing there
Draped in orange or
Spot light white

Blowing somebody's
Afro Blue Birdland dusk
Back into
Its riffed horizon?

The Wooden Floor

Kaleema Hasan

I want you to stay
here in the middle of the night
making love with promises
and prohibitions
I caught you stealing
red from the sun
glow from the moon
intricate, a moon dull
in a black sky, birds have
given up flying in the sky
I want you to finish
hurry, and be on your way
the sun wishes to set
prayers must be kept
gather this dress
by the hem pull it close
to her thighs
bare upon
the wooden floor.

Long Song

Kaleema Hasan

Desperately; and your spirit grinds to a halt:
disillusionment runs by every fifteen minutes
with the same trio, melody the same,
same vocal styling, as too the
chord arrangements
pitch, the guitar lick
the same drum roll the same dice.

Praying to My Dead Trinidad Parents

Lolita Hernandez

I need to pray,
but have no god
only you two angels
once brown-fleshed.
You two
were a couple of sets of laughing teeth
a regular pair of bakes and buhl jowl eaters.
Real funsticks shuffling side to side in
old calypso movements,
Lord Invader, for example.

You had the power to make my name indelible,
and you did so with juice from avocado seed
all the while filling my head up
with memories of pre-steel-pan Trinidad
for me to know you
as you were then
maybe singing off key
something like
Brown Skin Gal Stay Home and Mine Baby
tunes to sing while
swaying with a pot full of pelau,
some fruit and a little nip of rum
on the way to your spot on Maracas,
sou sou money already stashed.
Ah Trini have a rhythm way about them
when the sun is hot and salt water beckons.

There is no sun or salt water here,
and I don't know what song to sing
or memories to give my children
for them to carry on.
But carry on they do,
both with tattoos of Trinidad
boot-shaped in red, white and black.
I don't know how or why they felt compelled to

put a whole island on one of their body parts
except maybe it was you marking them in such a way
they could be identified
if ever they become lost in this mess we call a world.

So hear me now
I beg of you
since these two are with tattoos,
could you go where they are
with their big ideas and Trinidad colors
and watch over them for me?
I ent able.
Even if I could be with them,
I can't help them survive these events,
which are out of my hands.
These events which are beyond memories filled with
simple songs and island rhythms

Then please
appear again in my dreams.
Glide peacefully across space and time
behind my eyes in front of my brain
in the pit of my stomach or between my heartbeats.
Smiling always warm
like the island sunshine buried with you.
Even death can't take that,
even the nasty years of Detroit winters,
its musty stinking summers

Oh Lorse, I feel so helpless.
Look, I'm begging you.
I believe you have the power
to protest these two and their tattoos,
which is why I am praying to you now.

Right now.

Monarch Butterfly Haiku

Mildred Hunt

The Summons
Predestined flyers,
each in muted harmony
embrace their calling.

The Pilgrimage
Silent is their song.
Solitary notes strike chords
in winged music.

The Convocation
Home for the cluster,
migration south crescendos
a hushed codetta.

The Storm

Thoughts like lightning crack.
Thunder in my consciousness
drives me to shelter.

Dandelions

So much a nuisance
they defy formality
with random delights

Shoes

Stephen Jones

Oddly, I do not recall the fear,
panic from the loss of air, the flail
of legs, the burning lungs, the desperate,
useless fight to right myself, my arms
too short to reach sum-dappled sand above-
Above? My world inverted like the tube
that held me face-down till my father cast
his shoes aside and leaped in from the dock,
grabbed me in his hands, to pull me up
and out. I see, instead, the beauty there
in wavering light and shadow underneath
the surface. And the silence. And the sight,
when finally I burst into the air:
My father's crepe-soled shoes, adrift, upright,
waiting there beyond the dock for him
to step back in and stride across the deep.

Môre, **Mummy!**

Aneb Kgositsile

South African Maids, My Sisters

In the evenings,
they leave the wide stainless kitchens,
untangle themselves
from plump, pink arms and hands,
dust stray blond strands from their aprons,
and saunter out into the breeze
of each other's laughter.

They are stately figures
poised at the curbs
or seated squarely on the grass,
legs straight out in front,
with the walls of the owners' houses
a backdrop
to their daily consultations.
Together briefly, they review the details
of servitude,
confess how oblivious abuse has cut them
like broken glass in a sink.
They fabricate reasons to be gay;
count the rands they have saved
in knotted handkerchiefs
to pay their children's school fees,
or to one day have a house
of their own.

In the "free" space just at the gutters,
outside the mechanized gates,
and beyond the barking dogs,
they make strong medicine for each other.
They will live through the arrogance
of the children they nurse.
They will keep things neat.
They will not waste or break or ruin.

When they are alone
in narrow beds like prison bunks,
their sighs will rise in the dark
like a voile of prayers
above the big houses where they work.
"*Môre*, Mummy!"
"Good morning, Mrs.!"
"Yes, Mummy!"
The day begins.
The pink burdens clamor for her back.
There is the broom
the mop
the bucket
the heap of dirty clothes
the bleach
the iron
the stove...

(Môre means 'good morning' in Afrikaans.)

Ghost Orchids

Margo LaGattuta

There are ghosts that bloom in the night,
ghost orchids in the steaming Fakahatchee
Swamp in Florida. My late mother, a light
flickering in the doorway of her old room,
is caught in the corner of my eye, as I
watch *Sunday Morning*—a special
on John Laroche, the orchid thief,
arrested as he carries a pillowcase full of
ghost orchids out of the swamp.

Three knocks on the outside door;
I'm in a cabin haunted by spirits
of my dead parents, two rare orchids
who flew out of here but still return
to bloom inside my pillowcase at night.

They have no leaves, ghost orchids,
so vine-like roots entwine the trunks of trees;
roots of a life with Betty and Ed
wrap around me in this A-frame home
on a hillside in Gaylord, Michigan.

It takes years to grow from seed to bloom,
years to build a rare life like mine,
and now ghosts, hidden white flowers,
live in these closets and closed rooms.

Someone released the sounds of Electronic
Voice Phenomena on a CD, calling it
The Ghost Orchid. Sounds like strange
humanoid voices appear as if from
nowhere. A digital track of eerie words
intruding on radio broadcasts seems
like proof of electromagnetic life
after death. My father would have

loved those sounds, he who fiddled in
radio parts and stopped in his tracks
at a single note of Pavarotti's voice.
He told me once, on his last day alive,
If heaven's just a hoax, I'm
coming right back. I've waited
eighteen years and guessed, since Dad
was always good for his word,
it must have been real up there,

and now that Mother's flown too
(it is said that ghost orchids in
bloom look like ethereal
flying white frogs) I see the species
is a buoyant free-fall of love,
astonishing in its rare beauty,
and never quite lost to us, who tarry
behind in this hip-deep swamp of a life.

Outsourcing

M. L. Liebler

I had an idea recently. Genius!
I thought. I would disassemble the factory
Of myself, break it all down and start
To ship the most valuable parts to
Some other place. To do this, I had
To carefully detach each wire
And bolt and secretly unscrew me
From me, as not to grab anyone's
Attention or curiosity. For example,
While my foot was asleep, I sent
All of my memories south. While
My scalp prickled with beads of sweat
I sent love north, and later while my brain
Was entranced with commercials on television,
I sent those mysterious 21 grams of my soul
That I read about in *Time Magazine* straight
Out of this world—Way further than Mexico,
China, Pakistan or anywhere anyone has ever
Heard of. Gone—Vanished—just like that!

When all was said and done, very little
Of the old me was left. Yes, I had my
Ever growing fingernails and toenails,
The occasional annoying hidden rashes
Here and there, and of course—those annoying
Hairs that grow in your ears and nose at middle,
Age, but the substance? What was
The substance anyway? I wondered.

It suddenly occurred to me the other day that
When I gave all of me away, what remained
Was just another abandoned factory of self
And that's no way to run a life—

My Mother's Roses

Naomi Long Madgett

Meticulously she traced the pattern
on a pink silk panel,
oil-painted roses on green stems
of hope.
Some were buds and some
were full-blown possibilities.

It was the Thirties and times were grim,
but Mrs. Tilden's homegrown classes
in oil paint bottles, beaded lampshades,
and crepe paper costumes for pageants
in the high school auditorium
beamed a ray of sunlight into dismal corners.

In our back yard there were no roses, only
a profusion of sunflowers and hollyhocks that flourished,
summer after summer, whether showers blessed them
or not, and lilies of the valley that multiplied
with no particular care.
But my mother's artificial roses, painted on silk dreams,
remind me still of gifts too long forgotten,
of sources of sustenance too long denied.

Words

Yale Miller

breath's formation contemplation
parted mouth's reverberations
resound throughout the universe
thus return blessing or curse
reliant upon intent force and rhythm
when true say them

Stranded

stranded
awaitin salvation
divine redemption
burnt out transmission
tow trucks only come
if you call them

Used Books

Wardell Montgomery, Jr.

I really don't like reading used books
I have nothing against used books
I just don't like reading them
Now that last used book I read
I know at least three other people read that book
Nobody told me, I can tell
They left their thoughts in that used book
And that concerns me
One of them read in between the lines
I don't like that, I never do it
That's over-reading
Another one read more into the work
Than the writer wrote
Don't that just tick you off
Even if it were some poor, unpublished writer
Who was, no doubt, well read
Let me collect my own thoughts, thank you
Well that third one
You don't have to be a speed reader
To know he is a slow learner
Who must be a . . .
How do you say poor, ghetto kid
Without sounding patronizing
I can tell somebody made him read that book
And they didn't spend any time
Helping him to understand it
He wasn't focused, he was just looking for pictures
The syntax, the style, the premise escaped him
It's a great book, it could have
Raised his self-esteem
Enhanced his sense of humor
Even lifted him out of poverty
But I can't get involved in the lives
Of everybody who read those used books before me
It's new books from now on, my thoughts come first

No, I don't hear voices, I just read used thoughts
Yes, I want the cover to be nice and clean
With no dirty mundane petty thoughts
I do judge a book by its cover and thoughts
Now, like I said before
I have nothing against used books
I just don't like reading them!

The Doorway of Judgment

Schaarazetta Natelege

We stand before an impotent president
To profess his piety,
To guard his greatness,
To scream his success.
We stand in the abyss and bathe in holy water.
We embrace patriotism and drink freedom's blood.

We stand before this impotent president
To share bonds that transcend skin.
We are brothers of passage nailed to the corridor.
We are resurrected deaf-mutes.
We stand with hand-covered eyes in the doorway.
Of judgment.

Searching for a Dancer in Madrid

Sonya Marie Pouncy

in this city with no rocks,
i search for her: the
reason you will wake six more days.
so many miles from my touch
can a single kiss stretch this far?
the taste of your forehead, already
an elusive memory. the recipe
for sweet potato pie, already
shrunk to an age spot in your palm.

in this city, where gates
are useless centurions
(relics for museum tours),
i am looking for her: delicate
hands creating. *is this a question*
mark? or a movement
calling forth the oneness
of gods?

now there are no hand-made walls.
religion, as with children, is
more than god on a stick;
is as subtle as your inhale.
if i stand perfectly
still, will not i be drawn
by the rising of your breast?

i am now at the crossroad
where temples, no longer hoarded,
are given as gifts, juxtaposing
jesus, allah, isis and osiris.
can their wisdom brace
your fragile ankles? i am
still looking for her: a bright
dress with skirts riding the wind.

across the waters, we are all
dying of thirst. the blocks
of aswan have brought us
to this: she is not a nubian
goblet in the temples and she
is not a flirting veil in the basilicas
and mosques. i find her: a
piece of plastic airport art
smiling because all dancers
are *beautiful*.

Lament for fallen wonderfuls

Leslie Reese

In memory of Shysuane Taylor

lament for fallen wonderfuls

hard falling like trees
soft falling like dust
rushing falls, wonder falls

screaming falling wonder falls
quaking into wide and trapping walls
gasping screaming fireballs
drowned forever wonderfuls

bibles burning doubtful churning
from under rubble spirit crawls
brand new nappy caterwauls
throwing looping curveballs

in an infinite and dewing sky
full of twinkling for the eye

all my heroes: forgotten charming
listed in life's undergarments

sweet blues music trickster catcalls
shower compassion's waterfalls

dampening my soul, forever

wonderfuls

Holy Land

Rod Reinhart

Holy Land and Holy Shrines
Holy Wars and Battle Lines

Land of Peace, Shalom, Salaam
Land of bullets, stones and bombs

Mothers Grieving, sons have died
Demand their daughter's suicide

Fathers weeping for their sons
Give their other children guns

Here the streets where Jesus bled
Choked with dying, filled with dead

Land where prophets called for peace
Children beaten by police

Star of David, Crescent, Cross
Preach Victory at any cost

Ancient wall and holy mount
Body bags beyond all count

Endless prayers and praise arise
Calls for blood soar to the skies

Martyrs, murderers, soldier, saint
Stain the land in blood-lust paint

Land where murderous martyrs trod
Now blaspheme the name of God

Land where holy prophets died
Revenge and greed push God aside

Land where Jesus died for sin
Nationalist hate kills him again

Land of peace for every race
Bullets blasted in our face

Abraham, the father of three faiths
Longs that peace might be embraced

Land of Christian, Muslim, Jew
In place of peace, the wars renew

Distant dictators pull the strings
Bullets fly and hatred sings

And youth, before they grow or dream
Are taught to kill. Bombs violent scream

Even when peace was close at hand
They still drive strangers from the land

When will bitter violence end
When can enemies at last be friends

When Messiah comes, or comes again
Nations and Prophets force wars to end

And God makes all our hatred cease
And brings the Holy Land to peace

Mighty Warrior of Great Wisdom

Jacqueline Rae Sanchez

Mighty Warrior of great Wisdom
hear my words today. I come to you
from beyond the wind
looking towards the sunrise
of tomorrow.

The dew of yesteryear
has blessed me this day
and the vision of my cycle
within the temple of my being
has given rise to questions
not yet answered within the grasp
of comprehension.

The desert sand and noon day sun
hide secrets of shadows
lurking in distant alcoves of my mind
guarded by an elder
who desperately seeks immunity
from her past.

Would not the Secret Winds
gently caress my soul
and ask the Whip-o-Will to serenade us
con corridos sobre el tiempo
de la guerra dos del mundo,
y cancions de amor perdido
por el viejo amigo Jose Cuervo.

Drum Doctor

Semaj

For my beloved husband, Dr. James Brown

Introducing! Drum Doctor!
Houdini act of white-light proportions
clandestine vegetable lover
Disguised in a winterized neocolonial nice guy costume!
A crazy Joe writer of elixirs
You are a subterranean rhythm scientist
An insulated North Pole wardrobe escape artist
Wearing neon dashiki under stealth laboratory armor
under power house t-shirt
under chilly water like a pouting iceberg
under skin like the disappearing veins of Bermuda Triangle
Underground like a proud refrigerator
They tried to veto you
Those institutionalized mud pie slashers
They ordered you ink-blotted like Tuskegee Experiment
No wonder your scapel directs with suspicious passion
But you were Quark Fast!
Regenerating in the chant of a millennium beat
You sutured yourself after open drum surgery and
recuperated in the pages of an "I Praise You Black Woman"
poem
You the unknown anointed declared survival
and with the voltage of 6 million believers became...
"Poof!"
A reconstituted medicine blizzard
at zero degrees celcius
Now you see him now you don't
Endowed with such radioactive gifts from heaven
Cryogenesis of spiritual dimensions
An artic iambic pentameter
you were lattice stricken in a post emotional 1970's ice age
Hidden by shards of frozen mirrors
you became an optical sculptured illusion
made invisible to the bounty hunters
made invisible to the institutionalized mud pie slashers
but oh so tragically made invisible
to yourself

Drum Doctor of push button avalanches
may I candlelight your fossilized dreams?
Your prayer is a subcutaneous lava moan
that breathes swirling cadences through
the frosted tubes of broken stethoscopes

Your vision
a super natural velvet sleep
You yearn
to wade in the tepid vineyard of magenta sky
Ceremonial Ankh wearer
Testimony from a welded physician
From the sprouted tundra
Moon-bone connected to a glaciered heart,
Connected to managed fear in practitioner's silk

In your black bag
Is the answer to the thaw
to the thaw
You carry the illuminated brownest germ
You hold the bottomless tree bearing pulse
You hold the bottomless tree bearing pulse
You wear the generosity of capped mountains
of capped mountains

marked by biochemistry of burning genius
genius burning of biochemistry
You could have just melted yourself down
melted yourself down
but instead
you fashioned your geyser
into the fire black healing potion
From which I sip

Movement #3: The Bath

Sumarah

enveloped by you
warmest watery cocoon
transformed tears be sighs

lapping at my shores
slow motion shapes deep valleys
landscapes of my mind

your essence dispersed
washes away magnitudes
aches and pain of hearts

i float to the top
on silent beauty and calm
buoyed up by your mind

i swim in your eyes
pools of liquid brown, dancing
stroke and seduce me

we dip in and splash
sensualities immersed
ecstacies cleansing

we bathe in lyrics
evolutionary songs
whole, one we emerge.

Twenty-Fifth Wedding Anniversary

Hilda Vest

You were with me in the transition
when I shed the sashes of girlhood
and fashioned womanly belts
You were with me

One Sunday long ago
we abducted the ocean's scent
through windows of a narrow church
and made promises each to the other
You were with me

We invaded the beaches of Monterey
never certain though of the captors
Was it me
was it the ocean's song
or was it you
the cowrie of my universe

You courted me long distance
your fantasies safe
in flag-striped envelopes
The mailman never knew
the intimacy of his delivery

Then one day your black pearl arrived
never to return to its bed in Japan
You could not hear me swear
that it matched the pearl growing in my belly

The roses you planted still bloom
and spill hopelessly across fences and borders
in gardens where our children played
in seasons of their youth

Now when we are weekend winos
stumbling and speaking in tongues
I recall that you administered my first drink
being certain of its potency
Your watchful guard was anxious yet gentle
I grew silly before your eyes
and came to rest and to be born again
in your arms

You confide that you like my laughter
so I leave it uncanned on your nightstand
and hope that it will temper your sleep

We make love now not always out of lust
but out of good habits acquired
like warm baths at the end of crowded days
or windows pushed open after rain

Black Fascism

Rayfield Waller

(In honor of James Baldwin)

In Harlem
a brother
loved by his wife
and children
who holds a steady job
who fancies himself
above it all

swings a baseball bat
into the head
of a gay brother

who for his part

had studied James Baldwin
so much, with
such alacrity and faith, that
he thought he could come out
honest and real
right there, at the corner
of 125th and Lennox.

Post Reconstruction

Rayfield Waller

I look up
at a powder blue sky
which seems more lovely now
than it's been in years

as a quiet Black man
whose lifetime of hurt
is written in his eyes
asks me softly what it is
I'm looking at, and

I say I'm looking
at the sky

no jobs up there
he tells me.

If Grand River Were a River

Albert M. Ward

There are no waterfalls on Dexter,
but when it rains
the street shimmers like glass
and Oakman Boulevard
becomes a rain forest.

Blue and transparent,
the sky over Dexter
is bright in summer.
The sun washes the savannahs
and sidewalks in golden hues.
In a barber's shop on Dexter
I learned to play checkers.

At Parkman Library
my bicycle was stolen.
Had my African warriors
been with me, we would have
drummed on our shields,
walked through the tall grass,
and found my bicycle.

If Grand River were a river,
I would walk along its banks
from village to village.
If Grand River were a river,
children could dance at water's edge,
dances of freedom.

Grandmothers would say,
"Carry these groceries, boys.
One day you'll make fine men."
We'd walk Dexter sometimes
to Elmhurst or Fullerton,
or across Davison
to Clements and Pasedena.

Had lots of friends who lived on
Ewald Circle and Kendall.
The Grandmothers would tell stories
and give us lots of fifty cents.

I remember that summer of '67.
43 people died a civil disturbance.
Businesses burned on 12th Street,
houses on Pingree.
Tanks chewed up the alley
behind the garage of my Aunt Sweet,
looters running through her backyard.
Terror, tears, blood and ashes,
not to be denied.

If Grand River were a river,
trees would grow rich and lush,
like baobabs, their roots thick.
If Grand River were a river,
I would be free.

Woodward and the Boulevard,
marketplace, where
villagers and neighbors
come to trade and greet.
I see watercolors
of silk and broadcloth,
women with their bundles walking,
the elders with their sticks.

Mt. Kilimanjaro is bigger than
the Fisher Building,
with snow like crystal,
silver at its crest.
The sun sleeps there
when the moon is round and full.

East or West of Woodward,
I am home.

If Grand River were a river,
elephants could drink from it
and I would wash my clothes
among its stones.

The Children

We Clear the Land
(Cynthia L. Henderson)

The walk you're on takes you
Round the small
World of big-sister sentinels
Surrounding you,
Through the games you play,
Gathering fat sweet grape moments,

Poised, little brother,
only briefly still, you
Let the momentum mount to
the exact point that
Lifts you
Out beyond those walls.

Takin' Some of the Weight off John Henry

eilli Williams

We have to reopen
the stops on
the underground railroad
like Finley's Barn & 2nd Baptist Church
yes, space
where the grandsons and granddaughters
of Douglass, Bibb, Truth and Brown
can plan freedom
can plan revolution

Station tied together
by sun-dried vertebras
& gaping smashed skulls
missing legs & trails of
rusted chains &
rubbed raw flesh
packs of dogs
mimic their monster masters
both thirsting for Black blood
lusting for fresh human flesh
man-eaters, woman-eaters & children-eaters
classless ones
used by pseudo want a be aristocratic users
running circles on 4-footed beasts
around squares square dancing in revelry

Lynching lamp posts and trees
line the routes with
pickled penises in large dusty
formaldehyde-filled jars
hidden in basements, bunkers &
bombshelters
Yet on the same ground level as
lean-tos, root cellars and shelters
resting places
shielding spirited spirits

We have to reopen
all the stops on
the underground railroad
'cause too many people think
that we are free and
that integration meant liberty

We have to reopen
all the old stops
and open many new ones
on the underground railroad
ALL ABOARD

Dictate Freedom

Melinda Sol Wilson

I ponder on prior situations
Pushing me closer to power.
I am the product of a people prodigal that have been
Stolen
Sold
And are entitled to…
All of Earth.
I've established that extravagant and lavish life shall become
By studying
Tongues of native revolutionaries.
They've prepared me to sit down and…
Plan a plan,
And in this process practice the principles of the prophets,
Implement the Panther Party's Ten Point Program into my
consciousness…and
Master the craft of prayer;
Polish my poetical gift with grammar promoting pride and
dignity
uplifting our people,
Plant a seed beneath the soil of some child's soul,
Reopen reservoirs of consciousness,
Resurrecting the Bobby Seals and Assata Shakurs
that are lying dormant inside of us.
Release the Tarzan syndrome…
We've been framed to feel afraid to go home.
I have strong expectations of embracing the soft winds of
African shorelines.

In meditation to our ancestors' whispers that
God has given me,
With hopes that I can help humble some of these hustlers
enough to…
Sit down and discuss socio-economic issues,
Get them to pay closer attention to politics
And predict moves…

That Dictate Freedom!

Part II

Poems by Participants in Adult Workshops

A Salmon Pantoum

Jim Ahearn

In my hip boots, I step into the river.
The Garden is its name. Unusual, I think.
Salmon so thick it compares to Alaska.
So much nearer though to home.

The Garden is its name. Unusual, I think
yet appropriate, since it grows fish.
Fish much nearer though to home
Completing a journey by eternal plan.

Appropriate since it grows fish.
I am here to interfere,
Completing a journey by eternal plan.
I'll only keep a few, but play with many.

I am here to interfere.
Salmon so thick it compares to Alaska.
I'll only keep a few, but play with many.
In my hip boots, I step into the river.

Thirteen Ways to Look through Sunglasses

Jim Ahearn

1. With your eyes wide open

2. With your mind shut tight

3. Straining to see the trout in the shaded pool

4. Peripherally, not to miss the day

5. Imagining your destiny through the shade

6. Flipped up to brighten your life

7. Selectively to color the hue of your day

8. Into the stream of life to see the bottom

9. Ignoring them, when worn by others

10. Seeking a polarized perspective on my days

11. Fending off the unwanted glare of everyday life

12. Seeing what I cannot look at

13. Without fear but with humility

City of Dreams

Mary Ann Bozenski

Approaching the city,
Renaissance Center looms
through the mist;
built to revitalize
years ago.
Now new structures
blend with old.
Look around,
see the man
stretched out on the ground.
His belongings,
all his worldly possessions
lie close to him;
no shoes, no socks.
People coming and going.
To them he is invisible.
See the lights
of the Motor City Casino
late at night:
Oh! How pretty,
so very pretty.
There's a castle on the corner,
windows boarded;
majestic structure
waiting revitalization
in the city of dreams.

Accountant

Jill Elliott

Unlike his life
the out-of-control controller
attempts to keep his columns balanced,
calculates his profits, mourns his losses.

In constant motion
he taps the 10-key pad
yearns for his assets to appreciate
in value, straightens his paper-strewn desk

Adjusts cash accounts,
allocates ex-wives to expense categories,
juggles his numerous debts
while his dependents drain him.

Stares straight ahead.
Computer screen blurs his vision
as he contemplates the depreciation
of his lonely life.

Piano Potion

Lisa Leo Lanni

Eighty-eight fairies lifted her hands
over the bed that the
wee people rest upon.
Floating fingers,
like legs of the wee folk,
whimsically skipped across the furniture.
Merry music, sweet fairy dust,
sprinkled the air,
and I greedily drank in the magic.

Dinosaur Senses (Triceratops)

Michael Matuszak

To see a dinosaur -
its scales the color of forest
shades of brown green black
with a touch of bright flowers
its horns longer than I am tall
its body gigantic
its teeth flat for eating plants
tender and tough
its colored frill awes me
its movements amaze.

To feel a dinosaur -
its skin hard
feeling the edge
of every scale
its horns heavy smooth and sharp
its teeth with small ridges

To hear a dinosaur –
the rough screech and roar
standing out among all other
sounds its pounding footsteps
shaking the ground as it plods along
on its journey for food.

The smell –
of the forest air plants animals lakes
swamps and more mingle
with the slight herb scent of the dinosaur.

The taste –
in its mouth one of leaves, grasses and flowers
herbs and water hungrily
anticipating its next meal.

Toxic Love

Clarita Mays

I'm declaring
a state of emergency.
Our love has oozed.

The warning signals
lie cold, burned out long ago.

There's little worth recycling
in this emotional wasteland.

Tagging behind,
I sucked up your fumes,

wasting, holding my breath
under your suffocating spell.

I'm dumping the blues
and picking up a new attitude.

I'm clearing my head,
unclogging my heart,

making a new start.

It took two—me and you
to create this mess, but

I'm taking charge
of the Clean-up Detail.

Shop Around

Clarita Mays

It's all my fault.

I didn't pay attention
to the fine print
now screamin' at me
in **throbbing neon.**
He didn't warn me 'bout
the *void under certain conditions,*
the *limited warranty,*
or the *no guarantee.*
Maybe he did mumble somethin',
smothered over by
the unbeatable benefits.
"An offer," he said,
"too good to pass up."

So I bought in
and he moved in…

My lemon was disguised
as a sweet juicy mango.
I've tried to make the best
out of a bad deal,
but I'm runnin' outta sugah.
Won't bore you with the details—
the very ones I overlooked
before I said, "yes."
Got what I deserved,
buying' on impulse.
Next time I go shoppin',
gonna have my eyes and ears
w-i-d-e open.

Hamtramck

Ellen Phillips

Dense moving contradiction
Hollyhocks cover the forgotten
As feral children crawl my porch rails
laughing.
My dog barks at old men in hats
and bad jokes,
And we give thanks for Irene tortes –

Hamtramck

Dense moving contradiction,
Flashes of red
In swirling saris,
In dotted babushkas.
In passions above
the sullen debris.

dreams

Jane Sadley

we accidentally met today
on a crowded street corner
after weeks
of purposeful avoidance.

minutes passed
in a strange kind of slow motion.

we said nothing
simply looked at each other
feasting with our eyes
dreaming dreams we both knew
could never come true.

reaching out
you touched my face for one brief moment
then, silent, turned and walked away.

my eyes still caressed you
as you turned once
to look back at me
before being swallowed by the crowd.

too late
my hand raised itself
in one final goodbye.

P.S.

Jane Sadley

you're seated across the table

it's been such a long time
since we've been together

i can't get enough of looking at you.

gray now tips the edges of your hair

when did that happen…
i was supposed to be there
to watch time frost your hair.

too soon,
as you get up to leave
you put out your arms for a hug

still perfect

that place i fit.

the smell of you
will always make my knees weak.

my heart and hips scream yes.

P.S.
my lips say no.

Autumn Haikus

Deborah A. Sarsfield

September morning
subtle shift, introversion
softens us for fall.

One evolves like clouds
flowing with the changing breeze
destiny unknown.

Eretz

Susan Tawil

Come, my Beloved,
to a golden Land
where the air is heavy
with the scent of figs,
where the sky is deep and blue
and sunlight shimmers on the water.
Come to the Land
where dry desert thorns
crackle with sanctity,
where the earth carries
echoes of ancestral footsteps,
where souls touch Heaven.
Come back, my Beloved.
Come Home.

Red Plaid Mystery

Red plaid canvas–
snaps, wheels and white fringe-
stroller with two blonde boys.

Red plaid cotton shorts outfit–
silver-gray 1998 Honda;
she's next to yellow rose bush
in Wyandotte.

Red plaid cotton blouse with pockets–
librarian fixes internet,
and finds dolphins
in the stacks for five-year old Ashlee.

The Happiest Time of My Life

Ella L. Wright

When I was little more than twenty-two
I met a fellow I liked and he liked me too
Soon afterward, we married and had a few kids
When they became adults, they did what we did
My grandchildren now total high as eight
Their existence is my happiness. Life is great.

Part III

Poems by Participants in Children's Workshops

Children participants in Poet-in-Residence Program at Jefferson Library, 1992.

I Turn to the Earth

Robyn Sampson
(1993 – 2000)

I am Fruit

burst with lightning

glowing heart

rolling to a zero

Flowers all over icing

Birthdays, a round sweet fly

A doll and a zero

Semaj Brown and Robyn Sampson

The Awakening: Affirming Children's Voices

Semaj Brown

"Mommie, that's a poem! That's a poem!" My almost four- year-old daughter was referring to the words she had just uttered while poking me in my side, breaking into my 3 a.m. stream of consciousness writing. Tonight we were sharing my bed and Robyn had apparently just awakened from a heavily medicated sleep. I was thrilled that she appeared to be feeling substantially better. She sat propped against a pillow speaking the most poignant and haunting verses that seemed to be transported from the twilight of her dreams. Together, wide-eyed, we spied the alarm clock, counting the hours before she could call yet another enthusiastic listener, grandma. For Robyn, poetry had become medicine, the real antidote. When this little girl wrote, it was like inscribing sunbeams into her long days of dark suffering, which she endured due to sickle cell disease.

One Sunday afternoon, while in attendance at Broadside Press's Poet's Theatre, we watched as the clip-board for the open mic circulated throughout the room, bobbing from hand to hand like an unattended raft. Robyn harpooned the opportunity, signing her name in nothing less than a giant cursive scroll on line number five of the sign-up sheet. The conversation that would ensue between daughter and mother within the next few moments would be awkwardly wedged between rows of metal folding chairs. I was crouched down in a narrow aisle trying to convince my determined offspring that this was not an ideal time for her first public reading. I noted how important preparation was and that she had not practiced. I even questioned whether she had a poem fully memorized. Finally, I insisted that the bright lights of Channel 56 (they were recording a special) might make her nervous.

Robyn politely countered my every worry with a litany of buts, while Willie Williams, the director of Broadside Press Poet's Theatre, stood anchored close by and did what he so skillfully does – encourage. Yes, his miniature student of poetry was indeed encouraged and quite inspired. "Five, four, three," our discourse was interrupted by the descending counts of the public television director. My argument was out of time. I conceded. The film began to roll.

With a defined intensity, Robyn eased back into her chair. Her tiny hands were clasped tightly in her lap while her short legs dangled two t-strapped black leather shoes. Though she stared steely, straight ahead, there seemed to be an impish smile just below the surface of her severe expression. When they called her name, she sprang up and bounced down to the stage area so quickly that my heart missed the traditional opportunity to drop. Instead, I held my breath. The audience was adjusting themselves, shifting their chairs to look over and down at this very small child. The microphone stand had been lowered to its minimum height, yet it still towered above her head. The lights were glaring. The room was a captive hush amplified by the anticipation of the onlookers.

Robyn broke open the silence with the conviction of a serious artist. First, she began by stating the title of her two-stanza poem. Then she proceeded to speak; her words formed a conveyor belt of meaning that extended from her mouth to the hearts of the listeners. She concluded her recitation with a bow followed by a princess courtesy. The cheering erupted into the rain of proud applause. Happily she returned to her seat, plopping down beside me to a sea of whispered questions: "Who is that little girl?" "Did she write that?" "How old is she?"

Of course, I was a very proud mother who had learned a valuable lesson from that experience; but what was even more rewarding was to know that the confidence and self-esteem that my daughter exhibited had been instilled in hundreds of children who participated in the Poet-in-Residence Program over the past ten years. The poet/facilitators working in this Program helped to cultivate what was innate but too often left dormant in the individual. Self expression, a human need, was molded into the meaningful art form of poetry during a decade of work–shopping.

Through such classes many children and adults who would not have otherwise given voice to their silent thoughts have developed the poetic consciousness so necessary in these times.

Inside My Pencil

Anthony Asbell

I saw myself
writing a book
about my life
and about my
achievements.

If

Gregory Burns

If I were a plant
I would be a nice looking plant to see
People would stop by
From all over the world to see me
I would be tall
I would smell good
Like my father's cologne

I Am

Marvin Burns

I am like this window
I am clear and shiny
I am everywhere
I can save people
From fires
I help people build green houses
I help people see the glasses
I can be broken

Inside My Pencil

Sebastian Butler

In my pencil I see
words dancing around me.
In my pencil I see a sign glowing bright
that says write, write, WRITE!
In my pencil I see
my grandma's angel and Jesus talking to me.

To Those Who Don't Know Any Better

Brooke Cadwell
(Age 15)

Those who don't know any better come to our neighborhood
scared. They think we are dangerous. They think
this is a neighborhood full of thugs and people
who don't belong.

But I'm not afraid, and neither are my neighbors. We know
the crazy fat lady who walks to the store every day … talking
to herself like two teenage girls conversing
with one another …
purchasing only one item each day.

We know the man who lives in the scary house
and walks a different
dog each and every day … like a trainer at a petting
zoo, and never speaks to anyone who greets him.

We know the wine'o, Roy, with his foul breath and filthy
clothes who has something to say to anyone who passes.
We know the teenage boys, now young adults, who sit
on porches … having nothing
better to do.
They stand in the street
motionless, as cars go by.

We know.
We know.
We know we are in our comfort zone. But,
reposition the comforter, and find yourself in the unknown,
now immigrants lost in a country.

Untitled

D'Ante Chambers

I am like this eraser
Even though I
Erase things out of my mind
They will always leave
A mark on my life

Untitled

I am a stampede of elephants
When I stomp
I make a beat of music

Found Poem: Voices

Kenneyatta Cochran

Calling the wind
Those voices of freedom
Black Americans with their eyes
On the prize
Watching God and
Waiting for his return

If

If I were a color I would be blue
I would be like an ocean claiming the waves
I would smell like coffee in the morning
I would taste like a rose
I would sound like thunder through the night
I would be happy because
I am me
And that's all I'm trying to be

Grandmother's Death

Naji Davis

You gave me good love.
You gave me good care.

When I found out you died,
I ran to my bedroom

and cried,
and cried.

Sadness, sadness every day.
I cry when I think of you.

I know your age … I know some people need to die.
But you were very wonderful to me.

I was happy when you played with me.
I liked the way you laughed with me.

I loved to hear your whispering voice,
when you said goodnight to me.

Pain

Qydell Davis
(Young Adult)

My neighborhood is a place of peace
No fights or gunshots because
We are united by the team
A family structure of young men
From ages 4 to the late 20s
Sometimes we go to the movies as one
Some of our love goes deeper than family ties
One of our friends was shot yesterday
We were twisted with tears, great fears and pain
We all experience pain and suffering
Tears which are locked up inside
We look for joy in the heat of the sunrise
Looking for rainbows which smile
And wishing we could smile in so much pain
Explain this to the drug addict
So high he can barely remember his name
Some like kids who giggle
Go around laughing and smiling
But really all they want to do is cry
Why do we suffer sometimes?
Valid questions with answers that are hard to find
Life will always be a mystery
In which all will experience pain
But we must smile even in the storms
Or the darkness will prevail

The Five Senses of Me

Tierria Dickens

This is what you see
Beautiful and sweet
This is what you see
Short and thick
This is what you see
A taste of cherry and a smile
This is what you see
Brown eyes that always shine
This is what you see
Just plain old me

Untitled

Travon Godbold

I like myself because I'm different.

I have different eyes,

Different hair

And

I have light skin

but

I'm still **Black.**

Comfortable

Javon Greer

I am growing like a flower
I am a violet
I'm in my garden
Where the other flowers are
Daisies, roses, palms, sunflowers
They smell like fruit

But I smell like
Bubble gum
From Farmer Jack.

Brag

Benjamin Howard

I'm the best hitter in baseball;
I can outhit Sammy Sosa.
I'm so good at soccer
that I beat the best team.
I'm so good at dancing,
I'm better than Michael Jackson.
I'm so good at basketball
that Space Jam lost against me.

Brag

Briana Howard

I can rhyme better than Dr. Seuss.
I can write better than a typewriter.
I can fish better than you.
I can sing better than you.
Can you find a better book than me?
Bet you can't.

Summer

Sara Kinney

Summer is the best time of year.
It's filled with lots of joy and cheer.
I truly think it's lots of fun
when lots of heat comes from the sun.
Plus I think it's really cool
to get a big break from school.

Me

Darius Lawrence

Dr.
Adventurous
Running
Incredible
Unstoppable
Smart

In My Dreams

In my dreams I am a plane
I fly to New York about twice a day
Then I fly back to Ohio
To fly around and see the sights
With the light so bright
When I fly in the clouds
It's like flying by Cool Whip
And I love the sights I see
Like Cedar Point
And my friend's house
With trees, flowers and plants around it
And after that, I go on with
My ADVENTURE!

This Darn School

James Lee

Even though they can't see it
This place is a prison
Wrapped in a Halloween costume of a school
I go to it almost everyday
And get hassled and mistreated by my fellow prisoners
But the two good things about it are that
I found my best friend, Michael, there
And we have a lying warden
And we can do whatever we want when she's there

I think that the only time I'll be happy
Is on my freedom day: June 16, 2000
When I am freed from this God-forsaken place.

I Have Lived... I Have Learned...

Cassy Lemcool

I have lived on dance shoes
I have learned to dance
I have lived with anger
I have learned to love
I have lived with a cat
I have learned to sleep without moving my feet
I have lived with babies
I have learned to be gentle
I have lived to write
I have learned to accept refusal

Nowhere

Jessica Lemcool

Out in the middle of nowhere
Everything's so beautiful

Out in the middle of nowhere
Everything's so wild and free

Out in the middle of nowhere
I can't believe what I see

Out in the middle of nowhere
Now I know why nature is important to me.

Inside My Pencil

John Lemcool

I saw in that pencil
a lady with arms of trees
and feet of keys
with dresses of scales
that felt quite snakey.
That is what I saw
in that pencil of mine.

Animals

Henry Lowe

A lion, strong as wind
but his eyes are brown as my teacher's skin
Now the tiger, fierce as a hurricane
A rabbit, kind as a summer breeze

Mask

Tyrone Moody

When I put on the mask
I see a man getting executed.

I Am

Jamar Sadler

I am special in football.
I wonder if my mom will get married.
I hear a dog barking.
I see a toy to play with.
I want an X Box.
I am the best in football.

I pretend to play with toys.
I feel my grandmother.
I touch the chips.
I worry about the game.
I will cry if I lose my dog.
I am the best in the game.

I understand I do my work.
I say I behave in football.
I dream about my dad.
I try to play the game.
I hope my grandmother comes back.
I am the best in tennis.
I am special in football.

Untitled

Nina Sanders

My mom's hand is big
My sister's hand is small
My brother's hand is medium
My dad's hand is large
And my hand I don't have one.

Untitled

Tanisha Smith

Blue stars are speeding

like a car

Tiger king

speaks soft as a bed.

Untitled

Tiffany Weeks

Read us the bicycle storm

that tastes like juice

intelligent like an elephant

and as messy as the car.

Inside My Pencil

Shelby Woodby

I see N'Sync and their cute and smiling faces.
I shook them out of my pencil
onto my palm.
They performed on my hand
and I danced and sang so wildly
that they fell onto the floor
and they tried to get away,
but I got them.
I said I was sorry and I kissed them so hard
that I accidentally swallowed them.
But don't worry,
up they came when I burped.

I Have a Dream

Gary Young

I have a dream that my neighborhood isn't
Polluted.
I have a dream that my neighborhood has a rainbow
Sidewalk.
I have a dream that my neighborhood has
Time machines.

I have a dream that my community has irregular
Tools.
I have a dream that my community's bikes can
Fly.
I have a dream that my community has nice
Dragons.
I have a dream that things in my community are not
Regular.

I have a dream that my city rains
Pizza.
I have a dream that my city has shape-shifting
People.

I have a dream that my city's cars bark.
I have a dream that my city's people have
Magical Powers.

Editors

Gloria House, Ph.D., known in the African American community as Aneb Kgositsile, is an educator, poet, and community activist. She is Associate Professor of Humanities and African American Studies at the University of Michigan, Dearborn, and Professor Emerita in the Interdisciplinary Studies Department of Wayne State University. Since the 1960's when she worked as a student in the Southern civil rights movement, Aneb has been actively engaged in African American community and Third World issues and causes. From these involvements have come her poetry and other writings. Her publications include two poetry collections from Broadside Press, *Blood River* (1983) and *Rainrituals* (1989); a book of commentary on the political uses of environment in the United States, *Tower and Dungeon: A Study of Place and Power in American Culture* (Casa de Unidad Press), and a third collection of poems, *Shrines*, published by Third World Press in 2004.

Semaj Brown was a featured artist at the Toronto International Women's Word Dub Poetry Conference in 2004. She is the author of a collection of poems, *Dancing Shoes on Fire* (1997), and the acclaimed CD, "Tongue, Tongued" (2000). Her play, "Womb-Tongue," sponsored by the Arts League of Michigan and the Scarab Club, won standing ovations from audiences in 2003. Semaj's poem "Wave Rock" is the focus of artist Jasmine Murrell's art video "Wave Rock" (2004). Semaj has read her poetry nationwide, often performing with a full band, and her work has appeared in numerous publications. Semaj is also a science education consultant who lives in mid-Michigan with her husband, Dr. James Brown.

Willie Williams was born in Black Bottom, Ogun City, Detroit, in the year Willie Mays grew into a giant. As a child of the 1960's, he will never lose his idealism or voice in the struggle for freedom, using his words as weapons. A survivor of 10 years as organizer and facilitator of the Broadside Poets Theatre, he tries to teach others the importance of joining this struggle.

Contributors

Sarah Addae is a poet who lives in Detroit with her children, her step-children–when she can convince them to stay–her husband, dog, cats, guinea pigs, hedgehogs and fish. She keeps working to create the day when she herself is a poem. Until then, she uses the space between the words to meditate and recognize the amazing beauty in being.

Dr. Melba Joyce Boyd is professor of Africana Studies at Wayne State University. She has published six collections of poems and co-edited the acclaimed anthology of Detroit poets, *Abandon Automobile* (2001). She is the author of *Discarded Legacy: Politics and Poetics in the Life of Frances E. W. Harper, 1825 – 1911*, and *Wrestling with the Muse: Dudley Randall and the Broadside Press* (Columbia University Press, 2004).

Liberty R.O. Daniels is the founding editor of *P.O.E.T.S. Newsletter* and also editor of the quarterly newsletters for the southeast Michigan Chapter of the National Writers Union and the southeast Michigan region of the International Women's Writing Guild. She has performed poems from her, *I Feel Like a Kid* souvenir booklet in the United States and Canada.

Vievee Francis's work appears in *Callaloo* and the *Crab Orchard Review*, and other journals. She earns her living as a poet.

Joan Gartland came to Detroit from Brooklyn, N.Y. in the sixties. Her poetry has been published in various magazines and anthologies, including *Abandon Automobile: Detroit City Poetry 2001*. Her collection of poems, *A Passionate Distance*, was published by Ridgeway Press in 1991. She has served as head of the Art and Literature Department of the Detroit Main Library.

Aurora Harris's poetry appears in numerous anthologies and journals, including *Brooding the Heartlands* (Bottom Dog Press, 1998). She is a social worker who specializes in using the written and spoken word to heal and empower her students. Aurora is president of World Voice Cultural Arts, Inc. and director of the World Voice Literary Series at the Graystone International Jazz Museum. Aurora was also the coach of Detroit's National Slam Team winners in 2003.

Kaleemah Hasan is a poet, a fiction writer and community activist. She works as an educational program director in several Detroit area schools, creating innovative curricula to transform the lives of students and parents.

Born in Detroit, Lolita Hernandez's works reflect her Trinidad and St. Vincent Caribbean heritage. Her collection of short fictional stories, *Autopsy of an Engine*, Coffee House Press, 2004, is based on her years of work as a skilled tradeswoman at the Cadillac Clark Street General Motors plant.

Mildred Hunt is a Detroit native and a winner of the Broadside Press Poetry Writing Contest. She produced the Last Monday Blues Poetry Series during the 1980's and the Broadside Theatre at the Detroit Institute of Arts in 1995. Mildred conducted workshops in the Broadside Poets-in-Residence program from its inception. She continues to be active in the Detroit writing community.

Stephen Jones is a multi-talented poet, teacher, musician and journalist. He has worked as a reporter and copy editor at the *Detroit Free Press* and at the *Detroit Sunday Journal*. He is completing a doctorate in American Studies at Michigan State University. Stephen lives in Detroit with his wife, Colette Gilewicz, and their son, Alexander Jones.

Margo La Gattuta, MFA, is a popular Detroit area poet, editor and poetry workshop leader. Her published collections of poetry include *The Dream Givers, Noedgelines, Diversion Road,* and *Embracing the Fall.* She has won the Midwest Poetry Award twice. She has edited several anthologies and hosted a weekly poetry radio show on WPON. In 2005 she received the Mark Twain Award of the Society for the Study of Midwestern Literature for distinguished contributions to Midwestern literature.

M.L. Liebler has been a faculty member at Wayne State University since 1980. He is the founding director of the YMCA National Writer's Voice Project in Detroit. The author of more than ten books of poetry, M.L. is coeditor of the highly acclaimed anthology of Detroit poets, *Abandon Automobile,* Wayne State University Press, 2001.

Naomi Long Madgett, Poet Laureate of Detroit, is author of nine books of poetry. Her poems have appeared in numerous journals and 180 anthologies. She is a recipient of the American Book Award and the Michigan Artist Award, and an inductee in the Michigan Women's Hall of Fame and the International Hall of Fame for Writers of African Descent. She has received several honorary degrees, including a Doctor of Fine Arts from Michigan State University. The Naomi Long Madgett/ Lotus Press Archives were recently purchased by the University of Michigan Special Collections Library in Ann Arbor. Dr. Madgett is professor emerita in the English Department of Eastern Michigan University and publisher/editor of Lotus Press, Inc.

Yale Miller, a poet and scholar of African and African American history and culture, has been a teacher for 20 years in Detroit and in Kenya, East Africa. He established the Reproductive Health Initiative, an HIV awareness campaign with the youth of Laikipia, Kenya, where he lived for two years. He and his wife, Joya, are the proud parents of four children.

Wardell Montgomery is an urban folk poet whose work has been praised by educators and common folk alike. Many of his poems are rooted in the African American oral tradition of signifying, in which serious critical commentary is rendered with humor. Wardell has performed his poems at venues throughout the United States. He is the author of several chap books, the most recent being *I Loved Everything You Hated at the Jazz Club Last Night*.

Schaarazetta Natelege, a stunning dancer, poet and essayist, passed away in 2003. Born and raised in Detroit, and beloved in the African American cultural community, Schaarazetta was a graduate of University of Michigan, where she was privileged to study with the great poet Robert Hayden. Her poetry is published in *Solid Ground*, *Obsidian*, *HIPology*, *Abandon Automobile*, and in two self-published chap books.

Sonya Marie Pouncy is a Detroiter who received her baccalaureate in mechanical engineering from Purdue University. Sonya is a King, Chavez and Parks Fellow currently enrolled in the master's program of English Literature at Central Michigan University. Sonya won the Broadside Press Cavalcade of Poets Contest in 1996 and 1997. Her poetry has appeared in numerous anthologies.

Jacqueline Rae Rawlson Sanchez, a prolific poet, established the Latino Poet's Association in 1983, and is currently its CEO and director. Also in 1983, she became the owner/publisher/editor of The Sounds of Poetry, a press which has published many local and nationally-recognized poets.

Leslie Reese is an educator whose poems have been published in numerous anthologies, including *The Spirit in the Word, More Light, The Black Woman's Gumbo Ya Ya, Adam of Ife, HIPology* and *Nostalgia for the Present*. Leslie is a graduate of Alabama A & M University and specializes in helping youth to affirm themselves through creative writing. She is the author of the collection of poems, *Upside Down Tapestry Mosaic History* (Broadside Press). In 2005, Past Tents Press published *urban junkstar*, her most recent poems.

Rod Reinhart spearheads a writers' organization called the Plymouth Poets. He is the author of Spiritual Aerobics for the 21st Century. His work is included in the anthology, *Abandon Automobile: Detroit City Poetry, 2001*, and also in Broadside Press's *HIPology*.

Sumarah Karen Smith, a native Detroiter, is an accomplished singer, songwriter, arranger, visual artist, storyteller and actor. She has studied at the Eastman School of Music in New York and the Center for Creative Studies in Detroit. She is the founder/director of "The Art of Folk Tales," an interactive arts experience for story lovers of all ages.

Hilda Vest, a graduate of Wayne State University and a retired schoolteacher, is a previous editor/publisher of Broadside Press. A winner of the Detroit Women Writer's Poetry Award and the Alain Locke Award of the Detroit Institute of the Arts, Hilda has written two collections of poetry, both published by Broadside Press, *Lyrics I* and *Sorrows End*.

Native Detroiter Rayfield Waller writes for *The Michigan Citizen*, and for the online journal, *Corporate Mofo*. He is a screenwriter with the Zoetrope Virtual Studios Project. A professor of English and philosophy, he holds degrees from Wayne State University and Cornell University.

Albert M. Ward, a native Detroiter, graduated from the University of Detroit Mercy(UDM), where he was deeply influenced by Broadside Press founder, Dudley Randall. He has written verses for greeting cards and he is the founder of Your Heritage House Writers Group. His book of poems, *Patches on Mainstreet*, was published by Broadside Press. He is currently Writer-in-Residence at UDM, and is working on a CD of his love poems.

We Clear the Land (Cynthia Henderson) was inspired by her father to become a writer. She tries to go beyond the academic to meet the child's mind. Her poetry is included in the Broadside Press publication, *HIPology*.

Melinda "Sol" Wilson, a teacher at Timbuktu Academy of Science and Technology in Detroit, is also a highly respected spoken word artist in the world of Hip Hop, a genre dominated by men. Sol has authored *Spoken Experience*, a compilation of poems intended to inspire youth to struggle for liberation.